Seed Mantr;
Using Seed Mantras ar

Copyright information

Alon, Doron.
Seed Mantra Miracles –1st ed

Numinosity Press Inc

ISBN: 978-0692590102

Images used for Cover and content:
Cover Created by Shahnaz Mohammed
mailto:NAZNYC@GMAIL.COM
Cover image: Buddha sitting in meditation.© Wendy Le Ber -
Fotolia.com

Dedication

To you

INTRODUCTION

Thank you for purchasing this book, it is short but powerful. It combines two very powerful energy-based modalities that when combined can change your life quickly and with repetition, permanently. Seldom if ever have these 2 modalities been combined.

In this book, you will learn about:

1. Seed Mantras

2. Meridian Tapping

Seed Mantras, also known as Bija Mantras are root sounds in the Sanskrit language. They are, as their name implies, the root energetic sounds behind the entire universe. These Seed Mantras are the vehicle of power that when used properly, can help you make the required changes you need in your life. Mantras in and of themselves are very powerful and should always be used with respect and with your full attention. I created this book in such a way that it will be easy for you to maintain focus on the mantras.

The modern mind is overwhelmed with stress and distractions. These Mantras will help you Relax your mind.

The beauty of both the Meridian Tapping Technique and Mantra chanting is that you do not need to believe in them in order for them to work in your life. They are using energetic forces that are as real a gravity. One does not need to believe in gravity in order to feel its power. The same applies to Mantras and Meridian tapping.

I have divided this book into 2 sections:

Section 1: I will give you a brief explanation of the Mantras in this book, and how they can influence various aspects of your life. I will also give you some background regarding the Meridian Tapping technique.

In section 2: We will get into the practical application of the clearing technique and instructions on the Mantra practice itself. In this section, I will ask you to follow along in the text and audios if you have purchased them (They are not a requirement) . Each audio, if you have them will contain a meridian tapping sequence and the specific mantra chanted several hundred times. If you are interested in the audios please go to www.seedmantras.com. But they act only as a supplement and not a requirement.

I highly recommend you stay consistent with this practice. Although By Law I cannot make guarantees, I feel that if you stick with this, you can change every aspect of your life that you want to change.

Enjoy Your Journey.

Namaste

Seed Mantra Descriptions

AIM: Pronounced (AIM, like ready Aim Fire) This Mantra is the seed sound of creativity and intellect. This is a very powerful mantra and can literally change your brain so it opens itself to expanded creativity, enhanced learning ability as well as peace of mind. This is a perfect mantra for students. If you have a complex topic you want to study, this is the mantra to chant.

Dum/Doom: Pronounced (DOME) This mantra is generally used for protection. This Mantra is very popular since it is the root mantra for the Goddess Durga in the Hindu tradition. She is the Goddess of Protection. By using this mantra you are invoking a very powerful protective energy. This mantra is especially good if you want to increase yourself discipline and self- control. I use this mantra regularly to keep myself on point when I feel I am lacking self-control.

Gam/Gum: pronounced (GUM, like chewing gum) Gum is the seed mantra for the Hindu God Ganesh. He is worshiped throughout India as the God who removes obstacles in life. If you have an obstacle in your life, whether physical or spiritual, reciting this mantra will help clear it away. I use it regularly when I feel stuck. It really does work very well.

Hleem: Pronounced (Ha-leem sound) Is derived from the seed Hreem. It is, however softer energetically. It is used to bring an inner state of stillness. It can also be used to elicit a state of mindfulness before you speak. Often we can find ourselves about to saying something harsh, this mantra can help you become more mindful when you are in a heated situation. In turn, this mantra can be used to stop negativity in general.

Hoom: Pronounced (whom)This is a very important Sanskrit mantra in the Hindu tradition. This is a fiery mantra and thus has an energy potential that can both harm as well as protect. This mantra inspires and creates passion and vitality and can be used for both good and evil. In its positive aspects, it can bring divine protection and is very powerful in destroying negativity. This is a wonderful mantra to create a protective atmosphere in your home.

Hreem: Pronounced (like cream but with H instead of C) This powerful Mantra is known to have a captivating magical force. This is one of the most important mantras because it helps us rise above our delusions and ignorance which traps us from seeing life as it really is. Life is divine and due to our many distractions, we forget this. Hreem can help you liberate your consciousness. This is an incredibly powerful mantra and should be used with a positive intention.

Kleem: pronounced (like Cream, but with a KL instead of CR) This mantra is a very well known and powerful mantra used to attract spiritual and material abundance in your life. With Kleem you can attract love, friendship, peace of mind. People have used Kleem to attract sobriety and a clear mental state. If you have a specific intention in mind, chanting Kleem will help you resonate with that intention and manifest it in your life.

Kreem: Pronounced as Cream)At first, I was hesitant to add this Seed Syllable but I realized this course would not be complete without it. Kreem is associated with a very powerful Goddess in the Hindu tradition by the name of Kali. Kali has been misrepresented in the west as evil, but she is not evil in anyway. She is fierce. Meaning, when you use this mantra you are invoking a fierce energy. If you have a very critical issue in your life that you cannot seem to solve, or a bad habit you want to break and you have not been successful at breaking it. Using Kreem will help you break it very quickly. However, I must warn you, Kreem is not subtle. The results can be rather dramatic, but it will ALWAYS be for your own good. Recite with care.

OM: Pronounced as OM or AUM, long O) Is the most popular of the Seed Mantras. You may have chanted this yourself at some point in your life, either through a yoga practice or in meditation. Om is the primal sound. By chanting this mantra, you are attuning yourself to your true nature. If you want a deeper bond with source, this Mantra will assist you in achieving this state.

Saw/ Sauh: Pronounced (SAW like SAW) This is a wonderful mantra if you suffer from anxiety or depression. This mantra brings divine energy into your heart which elicit a calming happy energy into the nervous system.

Shreem: Pronounced (Shreeem) The Shreem prosperity mantra is a powerful tool that you can use to reshape how you attract and manage your prosperity. In the various cultures that make up the tapestry of human experience, we are constantly bombarded with mixed messages regarding what prosperity is. On one hand, we are inundated with how corrupt rich people are and that living a life of lack is in some way a noble existence.

On the other hand, we are told that abundance is a sign of being in tune with spirit and that lack is a sign of an imbalance. By Chanting this Mantra, you will attune yourself to prosperity and breakthrough any limiting beliefs you may have about money and prosperity.

Treem: Pronounced (as Tree, but with an M at the end)This mantra is extremely beneficial if you find yourself facing difficult and hostile situations in your life. It can enhance the aspects in you that are most associated with fearlessness, courage and daring. If you need to break out of your comfort zone, this mantra can help you gain this courage. Kreem can also help you gain these qualities but in a more direct way. Although these Seed Mantras are used for specific purposes, you may use them in all areas of your life. They will have a very beneficial influence on you.

These mantras work at the very core of your issues. Since all of your issues are energetically based, these Mantras are perfect tools to tweak your energy so it flows without interruption in your life. Energy blocks are the cause of all of your hardships, by clearing them; you free yourself from the bondage of hardship.

Meridian Tapping

Meridian Tapping is most commonly known as EFT or Emotional Freedom Technique. The science behind Meridian Tapping is quite substantial, as well as ancient.

In our bodies, we have many points of energy that run along our entire body. These energies are not only physical but also emotional. It has been proven that when we feel emotional negativity, it gets stored in our bodies. This is not a new concept; the Chinese have known this for thousands of years. It is thanks to Chinese Acupuncture that we know of these Meridian points. In acupuncture, the meridian points are engaged and cleared using needles. These needles are placed into these points, when the needles are inserted, they release the emotional and physical blockages that exist in that point. The beauty of this is that even if one point is cleared, it can have profound results throughout your being.

In Meridian tapping, the concept is the same; however, instead of using needles to release the blocked energy, we simply tap on them with our fingers, usually our index and middle fingers. Research has shows that by taping the meridian points, we can achieve the same results as acupuncture and in many studies; it has proven to be even more effective.

Since there are many Meridian points in the body, we will not be able to tap every single one of them. Therefore, we have isolated the key points that will be just as effective.

The Diagram on the next page illustrates the various tapping points we will use in this book.

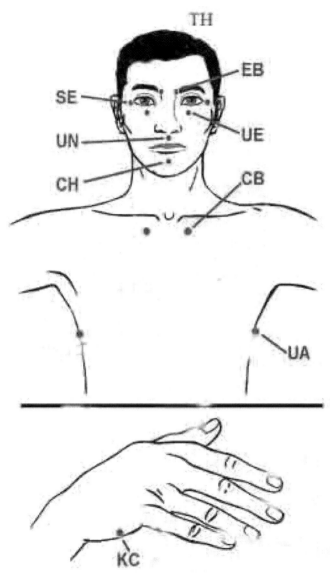

I know it may appear hard to believe that by simply tapping certain parts of your body you can change your life. However, it truly works.

Section 2: Practice and Application

In this section, I want to teach you how to use meridian tapping and mantra chanting. Please have the audios ready if you have them (Not a requirement). Additionally, please print out of the Tapping chart so you may reference it as we go. If you can memorize the chart, that will be even better..

 (When performing the meditations in this book, please dedicate a special time for it. Under no circumstance should you listen to the audios if you have them or chant these while driving a car or operating heavy machinery or participating in any activity that requires your full attention.)

Before you recite the mantras, it is imperative that we get your energy channels clear. In the next few chapters we will clear our energies and instill the power of the mantras in our energy body.

AIM MANTRA SESSION

This Mantra is the seed sound of creativity and intellect. This is a very powerful mantra and can literally change your brain so it opens itself to expanded creativity, enhanced learning ability as well as peace of mind. This is a perfect mantra for students. If you have a complex topic you want to study, this is the mantra to chant. Remember, you can use this mantra for any issue involving artistic ability, learning, memory etc. The tapping session below is just an example of a possible use for this mantra.

Let us do a tapping session to develop good study habits. Optional Step 1: Have the AIM Mantra Audio queued on your MP3 Player or computer, if you have them, but do not play it just yet.

Step 2: Take out the Tapping Chart so you can follow along during the tapping sequence.

Step 3: Think about how you feel about your study habits and measure how strongly you feel about it. Rate it from 0-10, 10 being very high and 0 being not feeling strong about it.

Step 4: The Tapping Sequence, please repeat the words below as you tap. Please use your index and middle fingers together to tap on the various points:

KC= Karate Chop Point: Although I feel my study habits are not good. I am open to loving and accepting myself anyway.

EB= Eyebrow point: My Study habits.

SE= Side of eye: This powerful feeling of not being able to study well.

UE= Under the eye: I feel that that my study habits could be better.

UN= Under the nose: I do not know what I need to do to make my study habits better.

CH= Chin point: it seems so overwhelming for me.

CB= Collarbone: How will improve my study habits?

UA= Under arm: Will I ever be able to learn how to study?

TH= Top of the head: I really want to be able to study any topic I want.

That is one tapping session; most people report that just by doing this acknowledgment tap, their anxiety decreases dramatically. Many people report that they are prompted to take action or have ideas and insights into how they might be able to get rid of their respective problems right after this session.

In some rare cases, the anxiety actually goes up. THIS IS A GOOD THING, that means you tapped right into the core of your anxiety. This means you need to keep taping on the issue. You should repeat the above tap if this applies to you. Now if you find your anxiety has decreased to a 1, 2 or 3, you can proceed to the next tapping session that reframes the situation in a more positive light and declares what you want to experience.

Tapping session 2: Reframing the negative feelings about your study habits.
KC= Karate Chop Point: Although I feel my study habits are not good. I am open to loving and accepting myself anyway.
EB= Eyebrow point: I intend to have excellent study skills.
SE= Side of eye: Studying comes easily and effortlessly to me.
UE= Under the eye: I intend to be able to study any topic I desire.

UN= Under the nose: I can have excellent study habits.

CH= Chin point: There is no reason I can't have great study habits.

CB= Collarbone: I know and intend to be guided to find the right study habits and techniques that will work for me.

UH= Under arm: I chose to learn efficiently.

TH= Top of the head: I am motivated now to learn and do well in my studies.

You should notice after this session that the anxiety drops and your motivation increases. It is very possible you may never have to tap on the issue again, the anxiety may be gone forever, however I recommend you do this at least once a day until you no longer feel the need to. It is amazing how powerful this is, the motivation you will feel will prompt you to take inspired action improve your study habits. This motivation means YOU ARE CLEAR.

You are ready for the AIM mantra. If you feel you are not fully clear, you may still proceed to the mantra that will probably help break the final block you have.

Step 5: Turn on your MP3 player or music player and start the mantra if you have them. If not, please recite the mantras in your mind. The reason we want to tap and use the mantra at the same time is to charge your energy channels with the positive life changing energy of the mantra.

That's all there is to it.

Dum/Doom Mantra Session

This mantra is generally used for protection. This Mantra is very popular since it is the root mantra for the Goddess Durga in the Hindu tradition. She is the Goddess of Protection. By using this mantra you are invoking a very powerful protective energy. This mantra is especially good if you want to increase yourself discipline and self-control. I use this mantra regularly to keep myself on point when I feel I am lacking self-control. The session below will be for general protection in all areas of your life.

Step 1: Have the DUM / DOOM Mantra queued on your MP3 Player or computer , if you have them, but do not play it just yet.

Step 2: Take out the Tapping Chart so you can follow along during the tapping sequence.

Step 3: Do you have a generally feeling of not being secure in all aspects of your life? Measure how strongly you feel about it. Rate it from 0-10, 10 being very high and 0 being not feeling strong about it.

Step 4: The Tapping Sequence, please repeat the words below as you tap. Please use your index and middle fingers together to tap on the various points:

KC= Karate Chop Point: Although I don't feel safe and secure, I intend to love and accept myself anyway.

EB= Eyebrow point: I hate feeling that I am not physically safe.

SE= Side of eye: I live in fear and feel unprotected.

UE= Under the eye: I can't seem to feel secure.

UN= Under the nose: I always feel something bad is going to happen to me or to someone I love.

CH= Chin point: it seems like I will never feel safe.

CB= Collarbone: How can I gain a sense of security?

UA= Under arm: Will I ever be truly safe?

TH= Top of the head: I really want to feel secure, but that doesn't seem possible.

That is one tapping session; most people report that just by doing this acknowledgment tap, their anxiety decreases dramatically. Many people report that they are prompted to take action or have ideas and insights into how they might be able to get rid of their respective problems right after this session.

In some rare cases, the anxiety actually goes up. THIS IS A GOOD THING, that means you tapped right into the core of your anxiety. This means you need to keep taping on the issue. You should repeat the above tap if this applies to you. Now if you find your anxiety has decreased to a 1, 2 or 3, you can proceed to the next tapping session that reframes the situation in a more positive light and declares what you want to experience.

Tapping session 2: Reframing the negative feelings about feeling unprotected or insecure.

KC= Karate Chop Point: Although I don't feel safe and secure, I intend to love and accept myself anyway.

EB= Eyebrow point: I intend to find my security.

SE= Side of eye: I am willing to allow myself to feel protected and secure.

UE= Under the eye: I intend to attract safety in all areas of my life .

UN= Under the nose: I know I deserve to be safe and secure in all areas of my life.

CH= Chin point: There is no reason I need to live in constant fear for my wellbeing.

CB= Collarbone: I know and intend to be guided to find the right people, place and circumstances that can help me feel more secure in my life.

UH= Under arm: I chose to take action.

TH= Top of the head: I am safe and secure.

You should notice after this session that the anxiety drops and your motivation increases. It is very possible you may never have to tap on the issue again, the anxiety may be gone forever, however I recommend you do this at least once a day until you no longer feel the need to. It is amazing how powerful this is, the motivation you will feel will prompt you to make the effort to achieve a level of protection you need to feel in your life. This motivation means YOU ARE CLEAR. You are ready for the DUM / DOOM mantra. If you feel you are not fully clear, you may still proceed to the mantra that will probably help break the final block you have.

Step 5: Turn on your MP3 player or music player and start the mantra if you have them. If not, please recite the mantras in your mind. The reason we want to tap and use the mantra at the same time is to charge your energy channels with the positive life changing energy of the mantra.

By the end of the session, you should feel a shift in your energy. Enjoy it and ACT on the inspired ideas you have.

Gam/Gum Mantra Session

Gum is the seed mantra for the Hindu God Ganesh. He is worshiped throughout India as the God who removes obstacles in life. If you have an obstacle in your life, whether physical or spiritual, reciting this mantra will help clear it away. I use it regularly when I feel stuck. It really does work very well.

The session below will be to clear any obstacles in your life

Step 1: Have the Gam/Gum Mantra queued on your MP3 Player or computer if you have them, but do not play it just yet.

Step 2: Take out the Tapping Chart so you can follow along during the tapping sequence.

Step 3: Are you trying to achieve a goal but seem to run into obstacles often? Measure how strongly you feel about it. Rate it from 0-10, 10 being very high and 0 being not feeling strong about it.

Step 4: The Tapping Sequence, please repeat the words below as you tap. Please use your index and middle fingers together to tap on the various points:

KC= Karate Chop Point: Although I am encountering many obstacles in my life, I intend to love and accept myself anyway.

EB= Eyebrow point: I hate running into obstacles every time I try to achieve a goal.

SE= Side of eye: I always run into almost insurmountable obstacles.

UE= Under the eye: I can't seem to catch a break.

UN= Under the nose: I always feel like I am being held back.

CH= Chin point: it seems like I will never get to where I want to be because of these constant obstacles.

CB= Collarbone: How can I gain a sense of happiness and fulfillment if I can't overcome all these obstacles?

UA= Under arm: Will I ever be able to have an easier life?

TH= Top of the head: I really want to remove these obstacles, but I am not sure how that will happen.

That is one tapping session; most people report that just by doing this acknowledgment tap, their anxiety decreases dramatically. Many people report that they are prompted to take action or have ideas and insights into how they might be able to get rid of their respective problems right after this session.

In some rare cases, the anxiety actually goes up. THIS IS A GOOD THING, that means you tapped right into the core of your anxiety.

This means you need to keep taping on the issue. You should repeat the above tap if this applies to you.

Now if you find your anxiety has decreased to a 1, 2 or 3, you can proceed to the next tapping session that reframes the situation in a more positive light and declares what you want to experience.

Tapping session 2: Reframing the negative feelings about encountering obstacles along your path.

KC= Karate Chop Point: Although I am encountering many obstacles in my life, I intend to love and accept myself anyway.

EB= Eyebrow point: I intend to find a way around these obstacles I encounter.

SE= Side of eye: I am willing to allow myself to be open to ideas that can remove these obstacles in my life.

UE= Under the eye: I intend to attract an unencumbered life.

UN= Under the nose: I know I deserve to be happy and I intend to be.

CH= Chin point: There is no reason I need to be encountering all these obstacles.

CB= Collarbone: I know and intend to be guided to find the right way to deal with these obstacles.

UH= Under arm: I chose to take inspired action and remove these obstacles in my life.

TH= Top of the head: I know I can defeat these obstacles.

You should notice after this session that the anxiety drops and your motivation increases. It is very possible you may never have to tap on the issue again, the anxiety may be gone forever, however I recommend you do this at least once a day until you no longer feel the need to. It is amazing how powerful this is, the motivation you will feel will prompt you to make the effort to take inspired action to remove the blocks in your life. This motivation means YOU ARE CLEAR.

You are ready for the Gam / Gum mantra. If you feel you are not fully clear, you may still proceed to the mantra that will probably help break the final block you have.

Step 5: Turn on your MP3 player or music player and start the mantra if you have them. If not, please recite the mantras in your mind. The reason we want to tap and use the mantra at the same time is to charge your energy channels with the positive life changing energy of the mantra.

By the end of the session, you should feel a shift in your energy. Enjoy it and ACT on the inspired ideas you have.

Hleem Mantra Session

Hleem Is derived from the seed Hreem. It is, however softer energetically. It is used to bring an inner state of stillness. It can also be used to bring about a state of mindfulness before you speak. Often we can find ourselves about to saying something harsh, this mantra can help you become more mindful when you are in a heated situation. In turn, this mantra can be used to stop negativity in general. In the tapping session below, we will use it to gain more mindfulness in the face of negativity.

Let us do a tapping session to become more mindful.

Step 1: Have the HLEEM Mantra queued on your MP3 Player or computer if you have them, but do not play it just yet.

Step 2: Take out the Tapping Chart so you can follow along during the tapping sequence.

Step 3: Think about your desire to be more mindful in the face of negativity; are you able to be mindful in the face of adversity? Measure how strongly you feel about it. Rate it from 0-10, 10 being very high and 0 being not feeling strong about it.

Step 4: The Tapping Sequence, please repeat the words below as you tap. Please use your index and middle fingers together to tap on the various points:

KC= Karate Chop Point: Although I don't believe I can react more positively to negative situation in my life, I intend to love and accept myself anyway.

EB= Eyebrow point: I can't detach from negative events in my life.

SE= Side of eye: This powerful feeling of being out of control emotionally scares me.

UE= Under the eye: I don't believe I can ever take negative situations in stride.

UN= Under the nose: I do not know what I need to do to find the emotional balance I need.

CH= Chin point: it seems so overwhelming for me.

CB= Collarbone: How will I find the strength and wisdom to deal with adversity?

UA= Under arm: Will I ever be able to feel balanced in the face of negativity?

TH= Top of the head: I really want to be more mindful before I react to negative situations in my life, but I am not able to do so.

That is one tapping session; most people report that just by doing this acknowledgment tap, their anxiety decreases dramatically. Many people report that they are prompted to take action or have ideas and insights into how they might be able to get rid of their respective problems right after this session.

In some rare cases, the anxiety actually goes up. THIS IS A GOOD THING, that means you tapped right into the core of your anxiety.

This means you need to keep taping on the issue. You should repeat the above tap if this applies to you.

Now if you find your anxiety has decreased to a 1, 2 or 3, you can proceed to the next tapping session that reframes the situation in a more positive light and declares what you want to experience.

Tapping session 2: Reframing the negative feelings about not being able to be mindful in the face of negative situations or events.

KC= Karate Chop Point: Although I don't believe I can react more positively to negative situation in my life, I intend to love and accept myself anyway.

EB= Eyebrow point: I intend to keep myself focused and objective in the face of negativity .

SE= Side of eye: I am willing to get out of my own way and allow negative situations to flow through me, instead of against me.

UE= Under the eye: I intend to attract stillness and mindfulness.

UN= Under the nose: I know being mindful will help me deal with any negative feelings, events or circumstances in a more constructive way.

CH= Chin point: There is no reason I cannot step back and assess my situation more clearly.

CB= Collarbone: I know and intend to be guided to make better decisions.

UH= Under arm: I chose to be open and mindful.

TH= Top of the head: I am motivated now to find the balance I need to deal with adversity and change.

You should notice after this session that the anxiety drops and your motivation increases. It is very possible you may never have to tap on the issue again, the anxiety may be gone forever, however I recommend you do this at least once a day until you no longer feel the need to. It is amazing how powerful this is, the motivation you will feel will prompt you to make the effort to step back and be more mindful in the face of negativity. This motivation means YOU ARE CLEAR.

You are ready for the HLEEM mantra. If you feel you are not fully clear, you may still proceed to the mantra that will probably help break the final block you have.
Step 5: Turn on your MP3 player or music player and start the mantra if you have them. If not, please recite the mantras in your mind. The reason we want to tap and use the mantra at the same time is to charge your energy channels with the positive life changing energy of the mantra.

By the end of the session, you should feel a shift in your energy. Enjoy it and ACT on the inspired ideas you have.

Hoom Mantra Session

This is a very important Sanskrit mantra in the Hindu tradition. This is a fiery mantra and thus has an energy potential that can both harm as well as protect. This mantra inspires and creates passion and vitality and can be used for both good and evil. In its positive aspects, it can bring divine protection and is very powerful in destroying negativity. This is a wonderful mantra to create a protective atmosphere in your home.

We will use this mantra to instill your life with passion and vitality.

Step 1: Have the HOOM Mantra queued on your MP3 Player or computer if you have them, but do not play it just yet.

Step 2: Take out the Tapping Chart so you can follow along during the tapping sequence.

Step 3: Do you feel that you have lost your passion for life? Measure how strongly you feel about it. Rate it from 0-10, 10 being very high and 0 being not feeling strong about it.

Step 4: The Tapping Sequence, please repeat the words below as you tap. Please use your index and middle fingers together to tap on the various points:

KC= Karate Chop Point: Although I don't feel passionate about my life right now, I intend to love and accept myself anyway.

EB= Eyebrow point: I hate the feeling uninspired in my life.

SE= Side of eye: I feel discouraged that I have not found my passion.

UE= Under the eye: I can't seem to be able to break through my lack of energy for life.

UN= Under the nose: I feel horrible about not having the courage to take risks that are good for me and that will bring passion into my life.

CH= Chin point: it seems like I will never feel that zest for life again.

CB= Collarbone: How will I find my passion, does it even exist?

UA= Under arm: Will I ever be able to truly change my life and take chances so I can live life with passion?

TH= Top of the head: I really want to change, but I am afraid.

That is one tapping session; most people report that just by doing this acknowledgment tap, their anxiety decreases dramatically. Many people report that they are prompted to take action or have ideas and insights into how they might be able to get rid of their respective problems right after this session.

In some rare cases, the anxiety actually goes up. THIS IS A GOOD THING, that means you tapped right into the core of your anxiety.
This means you need to keep taping on the issue. You should repeat the above tap if this applies to you.

Now if you find your anxiety has decreased to a 1, 2 or 3, you can proceed to the next tapping session that reframes the situation in a more positive light and declares what you want to experience.

Tapping session 2: Reframing the negative feelings about feeling lackluster in life.
KC= Karate Chop Point: Although I don't feel passionate about my life right now, I intend to love and accept myself anyway.
 EB= Eyebrow point: I intend to find my passion in life.

SE= Side of eye: I am willing to get out of my own way and feel vital again.

UE= Under the eye: I intend to find my passion and my meaning .

UN= Under the nose: I know I deserve to love life and I will.

CH= Chin point: There is no reason I cannot live life with passion

CB= Collarbone: I know and intend to be guided to find my passion.

UH= Under arm: I chose to take action.

TH= Top of the head: I am motivated, passionate and alive.

You should notice after this session that the anxiety drops and your motivation increases. It is very possible you may never have to tap on the issue again, the anxiety may be gone forever, however I recommend you do this at least once a day until you no longer feel the need to. It is amazing how powerful this is, the motivation you will feel will prompt you to make the effort find your passion and vitality for life. This motivation means YOU ARE CLEAR.

You are ready for the HOOM mantra. If you feel you are not fully clear, you may still proceed to the mantra that will probably help break the final block you have.

Step 5: Turn on your MP3 player or music player and start the mantra if you have them. If not please recite the mantras in your mind. The reason we want to tap and use the mantra at the same time is to charge your energy channels with the positive life changing energy of the mantra.

By the end of the session, you should feel a shift in your energy. Enjoy it and ACT on the inspired ideas you have.

Hreem Mantra Session

This powerful Mantra is known to have a captivating magical force. This is one of the most important mantras because it helps us rise above our delusions and ignorance which traps us from seeing life as it really is. Life is divine and due to our many distractions, we forget this. Hreem can help you liberate your consciousness. This is an incredibly powerful mantra and should be used with a positive intention.

Let us do a tapping session to develop an open mind and clear spiritual vision.

Step 1: Have the HREEM Mantra queued on your MP3 Player or computer if you have them, but do not play it just yet.

Step 2: Take out the Tapping Chart so you can follow along during the tapping sequence.

Step 3: Think about your ability to be open to the truth. Are you open to ideas that may challenge your preconceived notions about what is truth? Measure how strongly you feel about it. Rate it from 0-10, 10 being very high and 0 being not feeling strong about it.

Step 4: The Tapping Sequence, please repeat the words below as you tap. Please use your index and middle fingers together to tap on the various points:

KC= Karate Chop Point: Although it is often hard for me to allow myself to entertain uncomfortable challenging thoughts, I intend to love and accept myself anyway.

EB= Eyebrow point: My receptivity to new ideas.

SE= Side of eye: This powerful feeling of not being able to open my mind to new ideas and feelings.

UE= Under the eye: I feel that that I can open myself up to other ideas, but it is too scary.

UN= Under the nose: I do not know what I need to do to make challenging ideas more readily available to my consciousness.

CH= Chin point: it seems so overwhelming for me.

CB= Collarbone: How will I open my mind?

UA= Under arm: Will I ever be able to accept things as they are?

TH= Top of the head: I really want to be able to open my mind and heart to new ideas and feelings, but I cannot.

That is one tapping session; most people report that just by doing this acknowledgment tap, their anxiety decreases dramatically. Many people report that they are prompted to take action or have ideas and insights into how they might be able to get rid of their respective problems right after this session.

In some rare cases, the anxiety actually goes up. THIS IS A GOOD THING, that means you tapped right into the core of your anxiety. This means you need to keep taping on the issue. You should repeat the above tap if this applies to you. Now if you find your anxiety has decreased to a 1, 2 or 3, you can proceed to the next tapping session that reframes the situation in a more positive light and declares what you want to experience.

Tapping session 2: Reframing the negative feelings about your ability to remain open to new ideas and feelings.
KC= Karate Chop Point: Although it is often hard for me to allow myself to entertain uncomfortable challenging thoughts, I intend to love and accept myself anyway.
EB= Eyebrow point: I intend to keep myself open to new ideas, concepts and feelings.

SE= Side of eye: Challenging my preconceived notions of how things should be is getting easier and easier for me.

UE= Under the eye: I intend to be able to remain open and willing to entertain thoughts that may be in conflict with my childhood bookming.

UN= Under the nose: I know being open to new ideas and feelings helps me grow.

CH= Chin point: There is no reason I can't keep an open mind and heart.

CB= Collarbone: I know and intend to be guided to understanding

UH= Under arm: I chose to learn to be open.

TH= Top of the head: I am motivated now to learn and keep my heart open to new things.

You should notice after this session that the anxiety drops and your motivation increases. It is very possible you may never have to tap on the issue again, the anxiety may be gone forever, however I recommend you do this at least once a day until you no longer feel the need to. It is amazing how powerful this is, the motivation you will feel will prompt you to make the effort to keep your mind and heart open

to new ideas and to see things clearly. This motivation means YOU ARE CLEAR.

You are ready for the HREEM mantra. If you feel you are not fully clear, you may still proceed to the mantra that will probably help break the final block you have.

Step 5: Turn on your MP3 player or music player and start the mantra if you have them. If not, please recite the mantras in your mind. The reason we want to tap and use the mantra at the same time is to charge your energy channels with the positive life changing energy of the mantra.

By the end of the session, you should feel a shift in your energy. Enjoy it and ACT on the inspired ideas you have.

Kleem Mantra Session

This mantra is a very well known and powerful mantra used to attract spiritual and material abundance in your life. With Kleem you can attract love, friendship, peace of mind. People have used Kleem to attract sobriety and a clear mental state. If you have a specific intention in mind, chanting Kleem will help you resonate with that intention and manifest it in your life. I will provide an example of how this mantra can be used to attract love into your life.

Let us do a tapping session to attract your perfect mate.
Step 1: Have the KLEEM Mantra queued on your MP3 Player or computer if you have them, but do not play it just yet.
Step 2: Take out the Tapping Chart so you can follow along during the tapping sequence.
Step 3: Think about your desire to attract a mate, do you feel anxiety about your ability to find that perfect partner? Measure how strongly you feel about it. Rate it from 0-10, 10 being very high and 0 being not feeling strong about it.

Step 4: The Tapping Sequence, please repeat the words below as you tap. Please use your index and middle fingers together to tap on the various points:

KC= Karate Chop Point: Although I don't believe I will ever find the perfect partner, I intend to love and accept myself anyway.

EB= Eyebrow point: My desire for a partner.

SE= Side of eye: This powerful feeling of not being able to find the right partner.

UE= Under the eye: I don't believe anyone will ever want to date me.

UN= Under the nose: I do not know what I need to do to find the perfect partner.

CH= Chin point: it seems so overwhelming for me.

CB= Collarbone: How will I find a partner that is right for me?

UA= Under arm: Will I ever be able to feel butterflies in my stomach again?

TH= Top of the head: I really want to be in a loving and harmonious relationship, but I do not see that happening anytime soon.

That is one tapping session; most people report that just by doing this acknowledgment tap, their anxiety decreases dramatically. Many people report that they are prompted to take action or have ideas and insights into how they might be able to get rid of their respective problems right after this session.

In some rare cases, the anxiety actually goes up. THIS IS A GOOD THING, that means you tapped right into the core of your anxiety. This means you need to keep taping on the issue. You should repeat the above tap if this applies to you. Now if you find your anxiety has decreased to a 1, 2 or 3, you can proceed to the next tapping session that reframes the situation in a more positive light and declares what you want to experience.

Tapping session 2: Reframing the negative feelings about your ability to find your perfect mate.
KC= Karate Chop Point: Although I don't believe I will ever find the perfect partner, I intend to love and accept myself anyway.
EB= Eyebrow point: I intend to keep myself open to new people .

SE= Side of eye: I am willing to get out of my comfort zone in order to find the perfect partner.

UE= Under the eye: I intend to attract my perfect partner and intend to remain open to the possibilities.

UN= Under the nose: I know being open to letting go of my past hurts is what I need to do to be open to a new partner.

CH= Chin point: There is no reason I cannot find the perfect partner. So many people have found their perfect mates.

CB= Collarbone: I know and intend to be guided to the right person.

UH= Under arm: I chose to be open.

TH= Top of the head: I am motivated now to find the perfect person for me.

You should notice after this session that the anxiety drops and your motivation increases. It is very possible you may never have to tap on the issue again, the anxiety may be gone forever, however I recommend you do this at least once a day until you no longer feel the need to. It is amazing how powerful this is, the motivation you will feel will prompt you to make the effort to keep your mind and heart open to new people and activities that may guide you into the arms of your perfect partner. This motivation means YOU ARE CLEAR.

You are ready for the KLEEM mantra. If you feel you are not fully clear, you may still proceed to the mantra that will probably help break the final block you have.

Step 5: Turn on your MP3 player or music player and start the mantra if you have them. If not please recite the mantras in your mind. The reason we want to tap and use the mantra at the same time is to charge your energy channels with the positive life changing energy of the mantra.

By the end of the session, you should feel a shift in your energy. Enjoy it and ACT on the inspired ideas you have.

Kreem Mantra Session

Kreem is associated with a very powerful Goddess in the Hindu tradition by the name of Kali. Kali has been misrepresented in the west as being evil, but she is not evil in any way. She is fierce. Meaning, when you use this mantra you are invoking a fierce energy. If you have a very critical issue in your life that you cannot seem to solve, or a bad habit you want to break and you have not been successful at breaking it.

Using Kreem will help you break it very quickly. However, I must warn you, Kreem is not subtle. The results can be rather dramatic, but it will ALWAYS be for your own good. Recite with care. This is an ALL PURPOSE Mantra. Because it is so powerful, I will use it in this course for something very difficult to change. Let's use overeating and weight loss as the example. You are encouraged to alter this script to fit your particular situations. Please be mindful, this mantra should only be used when you have hit a wall and you need radical change.

Step 1: Have the KREEM Mantra queued on your MP3 Player or computer if you have them, but do not play it just yet.

Step 2: Take out the Tapping Chart so you can follow along during the tapping sequence.

Step 3: Think about your desire to stop overeating and to lose weight. How much anxiety does this cause for you? Measure how strongly you feel about it. Rate it from 0-10, 10 being very high and 0 being not feeling strong about it.

Step 4: The Tapping Sequence, please repeat the words below as you tap. Please use your index and middle fingers together to tap on the various points:

KC= Karate Chop Point: Although I don't believe I can stop overeating and lose the weight I need to lose. I intend to love and accept myself anyway.

EB= Eyebrow point: I hate the way I feel when I overeat.

SE= Side of eye: I feel discouraged when I realized how much weight I have gained.

UE= Under the eye: I can't seem to be able to stick to a sensible eating and exercise plan.

UN= Under the nose: I feel horrible about my health.

CH= Chin point: it seems so overwhelming for me to sustain a healthy lifestyle.

CB= Collarbone: How will I find the strength to avoid the foods I crave?

UA= Under arm: Will I ever be able to lose all this weight?

TH= Top of the head: I really want to be skinny, healthy and happy, but is it possible for me?

That is one tapping session; most people report that just by doing this acknowledgment tap, their anxiety decreases dramatically. Many people report that they are prompted to take action or have ideas and insights into how they might be able to get rid of their respective problems right after this session.

In some rare cases, the anxiety actually goes up. THIS IS A GOOD THING, that means you tapped right into the core of your anxiety. This means you need to keep taping on the issue. You should repeat the above tap if this applies to you. Now if you find your anxiety has decreased to a 1, 2 or 3, you can proceed to the next tapping session that reframes the situation in a more positive light and declares what you want to experience.

Tapping session 2: Reframing the negative feelings about overeating and being overweight.

KC= Karate Chop Point: Although I don't believe I can stop overeating and lose the weight I need to lose. I intend to love and accept myself anyway.

EB= Eyebrow point: I intend to keep myself focused on my goal to a healthier weight and habits.

SE= Side of eye: I am willing to get out of my own way and just take the steps I need to tale to lose weight and eat better.

UE= Under the eye: I know what I need to do to lose weight, now I have to lean in and just do it.

UN= Under the nose: I know I deserve to be healthy, if I didn't believe I could do it, I wouldn't want it.

CH= Chin point: There is no reason I cannot step on the scale and be happy to see that I am achieving my goals.

CB= Collarbone: I know and intend to be guided to make better decisions with food.

UH= Under arm: I chose to be open and mindful when I eat.

TH= Top of the head: I am motivated now to get healthy. I CAN DO THIS.

You should notice after this session that the anxiety drops and your motivation increases. It is very possible you may never have to tap on the issue again, the anxiety may be gone forever, however I recommend you do this at least once a day until you no longer feel the need to. It is amazing how powerful this is, the motivation you will feel will prompt you to make the effort to eat better and exercise more. This motivation means YOU ARE CLEAR.

You are ready for the KREEM mantra. If you feel you are not fully clear, you may still proceed to the mantra that will probably help break the final block you have.

Step 5: Turn on your MP3 player or music player and start the mantra if you have them. If not please recite the mantras in your mind. The reason we want to tap and use the mantra at the same time is to charge your energy channels with the positive life changing energy of the mantra.

By the end of the session, you should feel a shift in your energy. Enjoy it and ACT on the inspired ideas you have.

OM MANTRA SESSION

OM Is the most popular of the Seed Mantras. You may have chanted this yourself at some point in your life, either through a yoga practice or in meditation. Om is the primal sound. By chanting this mantra, you are attuning yourself to your true nature. If you want a deeper bond with source, this Mantra will assist you in achieving this state.

Let us do a tapping session to develop a deeper connection to source.

Step 1: Have the OM Mantra queued on your MP3 Player or computer if you have them, but do not play it just yet.

Step 2: Take out the Tapping Chart so you can follow along during the tapping sequence.

Step 3: Think about how you feel about your connection to source and measure how strongly you feel about it. Rate it from 0-10, 10 being very high and 0 being not feeling strong about it.

Step 4: The Tapping Sequence, please repeat the words below as you tap. Please use your index and middle

KC= Karate Chop Point: Although I feel my connection with source isn't as strong as I want it to be, I am open to loving and accepting myself anyway.

EB= Eyebrow point: My connection to source.

SE= Side of eye: This powerful feeling of not being connected to source.

UE= Under the eye: I feel that that my connection could be stronger and deeper.

UN= Under the nose: I do not know what I need to do to make my connection to source stronger.

CH= Chin point: it seems so overwhelming for me.

CB= Collarbone: How did I get so disconnected?

UA= Under arm: why me?

TH= Top of the head: I really want a deep and living relationship to source.

That is one tapping session; most people report that just by doing this acknowledgment tap, their anxiety decreases dramatically. Many people report that they are prompted to take action or have ideas and insights into how they might be able to get rid of their respective problems right after this session.

In some rare cases, the anxiety actually goes up. THIS IS A GOOD THING, that means you tapped right into the core of your anxiety. This means you need to keep taping on the issue. You should repeat the above tap if this applies to you. Now if you find your anxiety has decreased to a 1, 2 or 3, you can proceed to the next tapping session that reframes the situation in a more positive light and declares what you want to experience.

Tapping session 2: Reframing the negative feelings about not being connected to source.

KC= Karate Chop Point: Although I feel my connection with source isn't as strong as I want it to be, I am open to loving and accepting myself anyway.

EB= Eyebrow point: I intend to deepen my connection to source.

SE= Side of eye: Source loves me and desires the same connection with me.

UE= Under the eye: I intend to live a more mindful life.

UN= Under the nose: I can live as a radiant child of the divine.

CH= Chin point: I let go of all thoughts of disconnection.

CB= Collarbone: I know and intend to be guided in the right direction to get rid of this current state of disconnection I feel.

UH= Under arm: I chose to learn from source.

You should notice after this session that the anxiety drops and your motivation increases. It is very possible you may never have to tap on the issue again, the anxiety may be gone forever, however I recommend you do this at least once a day until you no longer feel the need to. It is amazing how powerful this is, the motivation you will feel will prompt you to take inspired action to deepen your connection to source. This motivation means YOU ARE CLEAR.

You are ready for the OM mantra. If you feel you are not fully clear, you may still proceed to the mantra that will probably help break the final block you have.

Step 5: Turn on your MP3 player or music player and start the mantra if you have them. If not please recite the mantras in your mind. The reason we want to tap and use the mantra at the same time is to charge your energy channels with the positive life changing energy of the mantra.

By the end of the session, you should feel a shift in your energy. Enjoy it and ACT on the inspired ideas you have.

Saw/ Sauh Mantra session

This is a wonderful mantra if you suffer from anxiety or depression. This mantra brings divine energy into your heart which elicit a calming happy energy into the nervous system. The session below will be to clear depression from your life.

Step 1: Have the SAW / SAUH Mantra queued on your MP3 Player or computer if you have them, but do not play it just yet.

Step 2: Take out the Tapping Chart so you can follow along during the tapping sequence.

Step 3: Are you suffering from depression and can't seem to shake it? Measure how strongly you feel about it. Rate it from 0-10, 10 being very high and 0 being not feeling strong about it.

Step 4: The Tapping Sequence, please repeat the words below as you tap. Please use your index and middle fingers together to tap on the various points:

KC= Karate Chop Point: Although I feel depression and anxiety, I intend to love and accept myself anyway.

EB= Eyebrow point: I hate feeling depressed.

SE= Side of eye: I always feel down and anxious.

UE= Under the eye: I can't seem to shake my depression.

UN= Under the nose: I always feel bad and don't know what to do about it.

CH= Chin point: it seems like I will never feel happy again

CB= Collarbone: How can I gain a sense of happiness again?

UA= Under arm: Will I ever be truly happy?

TH= Top of the head: I really want to feel happy and calm, but I just

don't see it happening for me.

That is one tapping session; most people report that just by doing this acknowledgment tap, their anxiety decreases dramatically. Many people report that they are prompted to take action or have ideas and insights into how they might be able to get rid of their respective problems right after this session.

In some rare cases, the anxiety actually goes up. THIS IS A GOOD THING, that means you tapped right into the core of your anxiety. This means you need to keep taping on the issue. You should repeat the above tap if this applies to you.

Now if you find your anxiety has decreased to a 1, 2 or 3, you can proceed to the next tapping session that reframes the situation in a more positive light and declares what you want to experience.

Tapping session 2: Reframing the negative feelings about feeling depressed and anxious.

KC= Karate Chop Point: Although I feel depression and anxiety, I intend to love and accept myself anyway.

EB= Eyebrow point: I intend to find a way out of my depression. SE= Side of eye: I am willing to allow myself to open up to more positive thoughts

UE= Under the eye: I intend to attract happiness and calm into my life.

UN= Under the nose: I know I deserve to be happy and I intend to be.

CH= Chin point: There is no reason I need to be unhappy or anxious in my life.

CB= Collarbone: I know and intend to be guided to find the right way to deal with my depression and anxiety.

UH= Under arm: I chose to take action.

TH= Top of the head: I know I can defeat this depression and I will.

You should notice after this session that the anxiety drops and your motivation increases. It is very possible you may never have to tap on the issue again, the anxiety may be gone forever, however I recommend you do this at least once a day until you no longer feel the need to. It is amazing how powerful this is, the motivation you will feel will prompt you to make the effort to be happy and less anxious. This motivation means YOU ARE CLEAR.

You are ready for the Saw / Sauh mantra. If you feel you are not fully clear, you may still proceed to the mantra that will probably help break the final block you have.

Step 5: Turn on your MP3 player or music player and start the mantra if you have them. If not please recite the mantras in your mind. The reason we want to tap and use the mantra at the same time is to charge your energy channels with the positive life changing energy of the mantra.

By the end of the session, you should feel a shift in your energy. Enjoy it and ACT on the inspired ideas you have.

Shreem Mantra Session

The Shreem prosperity mantra is a powerful tool that you can use to reshape how you attract and manage your prosperity. In the various cultures that make up the tapestry of human experience, we are constantly bombarded with mixed messages regarding what prosperity is. On one hand, we are inundated with how corrupt rich people are and that living a life of lack is in some way a noble existence. On the other hand, we are told that abundance is a sign of being in tune with spirit and that lack is a sign of an imbalance. By Chanting this Mantra, you will attune yourself to prosperity and breakthrough any limiting beliefs you may have about money and prosperity.

Let us do a session about getting clear about Money.

Step 1: Have the Shreem Mantra queued on your MP3 Player or computer if you have them, but do not play it just yet.

Step 2: Take out the Tapping Chart so you can follow along during the tapping sequence.

Step 3: Think of the issue you have and measure how strongly you feel about it. Rate it from 0-10, 10 being very high and 0 being not feeling strong about it.

Step 4: The Tapping Sequence, please repeat the words below as you tap, (You may change them to your particular issue). Please use your index and middle fingers together to tap on the various points:

KC= Karate Chop Point: Although I have this feeling of lack in my life, I am open to loving and accepting myself anyway.

EB= Eyebrow point: This lack in my life.

SE= Side of eye: This powerful feeling of lack in my life.

UE= Under the eye: I feel that there is not enough for me.

UN= Under the nose: I do not know how I will attract what I want into my life.

CH= Chin point: it seems so overwhelming for me.

CB= Collarbone: How did I get into this mess?

UA= Under arm: why me?

TH= Top of the head: I really want to attract good things into my life.

That is one taping session; most people report that just by doing this acknowledgment tap, their anxiety decreases dramatically. Many people report that they are prompted to take action or have ideas and insights into how they might be able to get rid of their respective problems right after this session.

In some rare cases, the anxiety actually goes up. THIS IS A GOOD THING, that means you tapped right into the core of your anxiety. This means you need to keep taping on the issue. You should repeat the above tap if this applies to you. Now If you find your anxiety has decreased to a 1, 2 or 3, you can proceed to the next tapping session that reframes the situation in a more positive light and declares what you want to experience.

Tapping session 2: Reframing the financial situation in a more positive light.
KC= Karate Chop: Although I have this feeling of lack in my life, I am open to loving and accepting myself anyway.
EB= Eyebrow point: I intend to attract abundance into my life.
SE= Side of eye: there is more than enough for everyone.
UE= Under the eye: I intend to live prosperously and abundantly.

UN= Under the nose: I can live an abundant life.

CH= Chin point: I let go of all thoughts of lack and scarcity.

CB= Collarbone: I know and intend to be guided in the right direction to get rid of this current state of lack.

UH= Under arm: I chose to learn from this lack.

TH= Top of the head: I am motivated now to take action to attract what I need into my life.

You should notice after this session that the anxiety drops and your motivation increases. It is very possible you may never have to tap on the issue again, the anxiety may be gone forever, however I recommend you do this at least once a day until you no longer feel the need to. It is amazing how powerful this is, the motivation you will feel will prompt you to take inspired action on reducing your debt and increasing your prosperity. This motivation means YOU ARE CLEAR.

You are ready for the Shreem mantra. If you feel you are not fully clear, you may still proceed to the mantra that will probably help break the final block you have.

Step 5: Turn on your MP3 player or music player and start the mantra if you have them. If not please recite the mantras in your mind. The reason we want to tap and use the mantra at the same time is to charge your energy channels with the positive life changing energy of the mantra.

By the end of the session, you should feel a shift in your energy. Enjoy it and ACT on the inspired ideas you have.

Treem Mantra Session

This mantra is extremely beneficial if you find yourself facing difficult and hostile situations in your life. It can enhance the aspects in you that are most associated with fearlessness, courage and daring. If you need to break out of your comfort zone, this mantra can help you gain this courage. Kreem can also help you gain these qualities but in a more direct way. We will use this session to develop courage to breakthrough your comfort zone/s.

Step 1: Have the TREEM Mantra queued on your MP3 Player or computer if you have them, but do not play it just yet.

Step 2: Take out the Tapping Chart so you can follow along during the tapping sequence.

Step 3: Think about your desire to getting in your own and way and breakthrough your comfort zone. Do have anxiety when you think about leaving your comfort zone? Measure how strongly you feel about it. Rate it from 0-10, 10 being very high and 0 being not feeling strong about it.

Step 4: The Tapping Sequence, please repeat the words below as you tap. Please use your index and middle fingers together to tap on the various points:

KC= Karate Chop Point: Although I don't believe I can ever change and leave my comfort zone, I intend to love and accept myself anyway.

EB= Eyebrow point: I hate the feeling of being stuck.

SE= Side of eye: I feel discouraged and weak when it comes to changing my life.

UE= Under the eye: I can't seem to be able to break my comfort zone.

UN= Under the nose: I feel horrible about not having the courage to take risks that are good for me.

CH= Chin point: it seems so overwhelming for me break my patterns.

CB= Collarbone: How will I find the strength get unstuck?

UA= Under arm: Will I ever be able to truly change my life and take chances?

TH= Top of the head: I really want to change, but I am afraid.

That is one tapping session; most people report that just by doing this acknowledgment tap, their anxiety decreases dramatically. Many people report that they are prompted to take action or have ideas and insights into how they might be able to get rid of their respective problems right after this session.

In some rare cases, the anxiety actually goes up. THIS IS A GOOD THING, that means you tapped right into the core of your anxiety. This means you need to keep taping on the issue. You should repeat the above tap if this applies to you. Now if you find your anxiety has decreased to a 1, 2 or 3, you can proceed to the next tapping session that reframes the situation in a more positive light and declares what you want to experience.

Tapping session 2: Reframing the negative feelings being stuck in a comfort zone.
KC= Karate Chop Point: Although I don't believe I can ever change and leave my comfort zone, I intend to love and accept myself anyway.
EB= Eyebrow point: I intend to lean into my goals and breakout of my comfort zone.
SE= Side of eye: I am willing to get out of my own way.

UE= Under the eye: I know what I need to do to, I just need to do it.

 UN= Under the nose: I know I deserve good things.

CH= Chin point: There is no reason I cannot step out of my comfort zone.

CB= Collarbone: I know and intend to be guided to make better decisions and breakthrough my own SELF IMPOSED limitations.

UH= Under arm: I chose to take action.

TH= Top of the head: I am motivated, let's do it.

You should notice after this session that the anxiety drops and your motivation increases. It is very possible you may never have to tap on the issue again, the anxiety may be gone forever, however I recommend you do this at least once a day until you no longer feel the need to. It is amazing how powerful this is, the motivation you will feel will prompt you to make the effort to embrace change and get out of your comfort zone. This motivation means YOU ARE CLEAR. You are ready for the TREEM mantra. If you feel you are not fully clear, you may still proceed to the mantra that will probably help break the final block you have.

Step 5: Turn on your MP3 player or music player and start the mantra if you have them. If not please recite the mantras in your mind. The reason we want to tap and use the mantra at the same time is to charge your energy channels with the positive life changing energy of the mantra.

By the end of the session, you should feel a shift in your energy. Enjoy it and ACT on the inspired ideas you have.

Conclusion

I want to thank you for purchasing this book. If you take the time and effort to practice the techniques in it you can radically change your life for the better in a very short period. If you have any questions; please feel free to email me at doron@numinositypress.com

I wish you peace and prosperity.

Namaste,

Doron

For other life changing books please visit my author page : amazon.com/author/doronalon

About The Author

Doron Alon is a bestselling author of 50 books in 6 genres and is founder of Numinosity Press Inc.

He writes on a wide variety of topics including History, Self-help, Self-Publishing, and Spirituality. Doron's background and 24 years of experience in meditation training, Meridian tapping (also known as E.F.T), Subliminal Messaging and other modalities has made him a much sought after expert in the self help and spirituality fields. His conversational writing style and his ability to take complex topics and make them easily accessible has gained him popularity in the genres that he writes for.

To learn more about his other books on a wide variety of topics please visit doronalon.com or visit his author page at Amazon to find out more. If you have any questions, please feel free to email him at doron@numinositypress.com

Please explore his other books here:

amazon.com/author/doronalon

Disclaimer:

By law, I need to add this statement. This audio and book are for educational purposes only and does not claim to prevent or cure any disease. The advice and methods in this audio and booklet should not be construed as financial advice. Please seek advice from a professional financial adviser regarding your financial situation.

By purchasing and listening to this book, you understand that results are not guaranteed. In light of this, you understand that in the unlikely event that this audio or book does not work or causes harm in any area of your life, you agree that you do not hold Doron Alon, Numinosity Press Inc, its employees or affiliates liable for any damages you may experience or incur.

The Text and Audio in this course are copyrighted 2013 by Numinosity Press Incorporated. Reproduction or distribution.

15600511R00044

Printed in Great Britain
by Amazon